Contents

Uniquely
Tennessee

To be unique is to be special and unusual. Tennessee is unique. It is a land of high mountains, including those in and around the Great Smoky Mountains National Park, and low plains, like those near the banks of the Mississippi River. The state is home to both country music and the **blues** and has a long and full history that includes being the home of three U.S. presidents.

ORIGIN OF THE STATE'S NAME

The Cherokee gave Tennessee its name. One of their main villages was called "Tanasi." When European settlers moved to Cherokee lands in the 1700s, they used the word to describe a major river in the area and the lands that river runs through.

MAJOR CITIES

Each of Tennessee's three major cities is located on one of the three major rivers that flow through the state.

Nashville, located on the Cumberland River, is the state's capital and its second largest city, with more than 540,000

Memphis is named after a city in ancient Egypt. The pyramid in the Memphis skyline was modeled after Egypt's pyramids. Memphis's pyramid is actually a sports arena.

Uniquely
Tennessee

Adam McClellan

Heinemann Library
Chicago, Illinois

10/04
WJ

© 2004 Heinemann Library
a division of Reed Elsevier Inc.
Chicago, Illinois

Customer Service   888-454-2279

Visit our website at www.heinemannlibrary.com

Designed by Heinemann Library
Printed in China by WKT Company Limited.

08 07 06 05 04
10 9 8 7 6 5 4 3 2 1

**Library of Congress
Cataloging-in-Publication Data**

McClellan, Adam, 1971–
  Uniquely Tennessee / Adam McClellan.
      p. cm.—(State studies)
Summary: Examines what makes Tennessee unique,
including its landscape, people, music, and history.
Includes bibliographical references and index.
  ISBN 1-4034-4497-8 (lib. bdg.) —
ISBN 1-4034-4512-5 (pbk.)
  1. Tennessee—Juvenile literature. [1. Tennessee.]
I. Title. II. Series.
  F436.3.M35 2003
  976.8—dc21

                                    2003008984

Cover Pictures

Top (left to right) Graceland in Memphis,
Tennessee state flag, steamboat, performers
at the Grand Ole Opry in Nashville
Main Great Smoky Mountains

Acknowledgments
Development and photo research by
BOOK BUILDERS LLC

The author and publishers are grateful to the
following for permission to reproduce copyright
material:

Cover photographs by (top, L-R): Philip Gould/
Corbis; Jed DeKalb/Courtesy Tennessee Tourist
Development; Nathan Benn/Corbis; Kevin Fleming/
Corbis; W. Cody/Corbis.

Photo Credits Title page (L-R): Courtesy Tennessee
Tourist Development; State of Tennessee Photo
Services; Jed DeKalb/Courtesy Tennessee Tourist
Development; Contents page: Nathan Benn/Corbis;
pp. 4, 38 Andre Jenny/Alamy; pp. 5, 10, 11T, 13T,
13B, 14T Jed DeKalb/Courtesy Tennessee Tourist
Development; pp. 7, 39, 45 maps by IMA for Book
Builders LLC; p. 8 Brand X Pictures/Alamy; pp. 9, 30
Barbara Minton/Heinemann Library; p. 13M Joy
Spur/Bruce Coleman Inc; p. 14M Kenneth
Deitcher/Bruce Coleman Inc; p. 14B Joe McDonald/
Bruce Coleman Inc; p. 15T Phil A. Dotson/Photo
Researchers Inc; p. 15B Kaj R. Svensson/Photo Re-
searchers Inc; pp. 16T, 21T, 26, 28, 29, 34, 41, 44
Courtesy Tennessee Tourist Development; pp. 17, 19,
20, 21B, 22T, Culver Pictures; p. 22B Hulton Getty;
p. 23 Kevin Fleming/Corbis; p. 26 State of Tennessee
Photo Services; p. 33 R. Capozzelli for Heinemann
Library; p. 35 Elsa/Staff/Getty; p. 36 Stock Connec-
tion, Inc/Alamy; p. 37T Gene Ahrens/Bruce Coleman
Inc; p. 37B Courtesy of Federal Express; p. 40 Philip
Gould/Corbis; p. 42 W. Cody/Corbis.

Special thanks to Renee Lyn Graves of the
University of Memphis for her expert comments
in the preparation of this book.

Every effort has been made to contact copyright
holders of any material reproduced in this book.
Any omissions will be rectified in subsequent
printings if notice is given to the publisher.

Some words are shown in bold, **like this.**
You can find out what they mean by looking
in the glossary.

people. It is also the capital of country music, home to attractions such as the Grand Ole Opry and the Country Music Hall of Fame. More country music is recorded in Nashville than anywhere else in the world.

Memphis is Tennessee's biggest city in terms of population—650,000 people live there. It lies in the far western part of the state, on **bluffs** overlooking the Mississippi River. Today, FedEx, the express delivery service, has its world headquarters there.

Knoxville is the largest city in eastern Tennessee. Established in 1791, it now has more than 170,000 residents. Located on the Tennessee River, Knoxville is the home of the University of Tennessee. It is also the headquarters of the Tennessee Valley Authority, a government agency established in 1933 to bring inexpensive **hydroelectric power** to Tennessee and surrounding states.

Lookout Mountain

Lookout Mountain, near Chattanooga in the southeastern corner of the state, has a view of seven states. From its top on a clear day you can see the states of Tennessee, Georgia, Alabama, North Carolina, South Carolina, Virginia, and Kentucky. The Seven States Flag Court on top of Lookout

Mountain pays tribute to the states visible from the mountaintop. The mountain rises to an elevation of more than 2,000 feet.

Tennessee's Geography and Climate

The long state of Tennessee borders Kentucky and Virginia to the north. On the east, the state borders North Carolina, while to the south it touches Georgia, Alabama, and Mississippi. Tennessee shares borders across the Mississippi River with Missouri and Arkansas.

Tennessee can be divided into three main geographical regions: West, Middle, and East. These regions are also known as the three Grand Divisions of Tennessee. The three regions have enough differences in geography and climate that road signs at Tennessee's borders used to welcome visitors to "the Three States of Tennessee."

LAND

West Tennessee is flat and is drained by slow-moving creeks that flow into the Mississippi River. Near the Mississippi, you can find Reelfoot Lake, Tennessee's only naturally occurring lake. In Middle Tennessee you can find rolling hills and valleys, as well as the winding Cumberland River. East Ten-

The East Tennessee mountains are the snowiest part of the state, averaging about ten inches of snow a year.

Average Annual Precipitation
Tennessee

Precipitation in inches
- Less than 44
- 44 to 50
- 50 to 56
- 56 to 64
- above 64

★ Capital
• City

nessee is mountainous. The Appalachian Mountains form the eastern border of the state. Clingman's Dome, the highest peak in the state, rises to 6,643 feet.

CLIMATE

When it comes to weather, Tennessee has a little of everything! For hot, steamy weather, visit Memphis in August, where temperatures can reach 100°F and higher. To play in the snow, take a trip to East Tennessee and visit the Great Smoky Mountains National Park in wintertime.

Tennessee has a **temperate** climate. At the same time, Tennesseans get to experience the change of seasons. Summer temperatures in Tennessee range from warm to hot. Daytime temperatures usually run in the 80s and 90s. Air cools as it rises, so temperatures in Memphis are much warmer than in the hilly and mountainous parts of eastern and central Tennessee. Winters are usually cool, with average temperatures in the 30s and 40s throughout much of the state, though often it can get much colder.

PRECIPITATION—RAIN AND SNOW

Overall, Tennessee gets a good, steady stream of **precipitation.** The wettest parts of the state are in the mountains, near the Great Smoky Mountains National Park. Oddly enough, the driest part of Tennessee is also in the mountains, near the cities of Bristol and Kingsport.

Tennessee's statewide average precipitation is approximately 50 inches a year, with the driest areas getting around 40 inches and the wettest areas getting more than 80 inches.

Famous Firsts

AFRICAN AMERICAN BUSINESSES

Nashville is home to two pioneering African American businesses. In 1922 Moses and Calvin McKissack founded McKissack and McKissack, the oldest African American architectural firm in the United States. In addition, Citizens Savings Bank and Trust Company is the nation's oldest African American financial institution. Members of the Negro Business League of Nashville founded the bank in 1904 to serve the African American community.

RUBY FALLS

Ruby Falls, located inside Lookout Mountain near Chattanooga, is the world's highest waterfall completely beneath the earth's surface. Leo Lambert, a local cave explorer and businessman, discovered the falls in 1928. He named it after his wife, Ruby. Ruby Falls drops 145 feet within the mountain. Water from the falls eventually makes its way above ground and flows into the Tennessee River.

MINIATURE GOLF

Garnet Carter developed miniature golf on Lookout Mountain in 1926. He called the game "Tom Thumb

More than 70 years after Garnet Carter opened his miniature golf course on Lookout Mountain, the game remains popular.

8

Golf," after a fairy-tale character who was very small. Carter's miniature golf course challenged people to putt a ball into a hole by going through pipes and around obstacles such as rocks and statues of elves. He hoped it would bring more people to the full-sized golf course that he ran on Lookout Mountain. To his surprise, more people wanted to play miniature golf than play the real game!

COCA-COLA BOTTLING

Today, bottles of Coca-Cola, or Coke, are sold almost everywhere. Bottled Coke got its official start in Chattanooga in 1899. Businessmen J.B. Whitehead and Ben Thomas bought the rights to bottle and sell Coke, which was a popular soda fountain drink at the time. They paid just $1 for those rights—less than the cost of a single two-liter bottle of Coke today. The Chattanooga Coca-Cola Bottling Company, which celebrated 100 years in business in 1999, is still going strong.

THE SELF-SERVICE GROCERY STORE

In Memphis in 1916, Clarence Saunders opened the first self-service grocery store. He named the store Piggly Wiggly, thinking it was a name that would stick in people's minds. At the Piggly Wiggly, customers picked out their own groceries. Earlier, customers handed their grocery lists to clerks who would collect the food for them. Piggly Wiggly also had the first store with checkout stands and a price on every item. There are still more than 600 Piggly Wiggly stores in business today.

At Piggly Wiggly stores, shoppers serve themselves.

Today, visitors can take boat tours of the Lost Sea. The tours last one hour, and sometimes the boats have glass bottoms.

THE LOST SEA

In Craighead Caverns near Sweetwater is the Lost Sea. At about 800 feet long and 220 feet wide, it is the world's largest underground lake. Ben Sands, a 13-year-old boy, discovered it in 1905. Sands squeezed through a hole 300 feet underground and found himself in a gigantic room with water in all directions.

NUCLEAR REACTOR

Tennessee was also the site of an important scientific first. On November 4, 1943, the Graphite Reactor at Oak Ridge National Laboratory became the first continually operated **nuclear reactor** in the world. The U.S. government built the reactor during **World War II** (1939–1945) to produce **uranium** and **plutonium**—materials that could be used to make an **atom bomb.** It also was the first reactor in the world to produce electricity from **nuclear energy.**

Tennessee's State Symbols

TENNESSEE STATE FLAG

Tennessee's flag was adopted in 1905. It was designed by LeRoy Reeves of Johnson City. The three stars stand for the three Grand Divisions of the state. The blue circle symbolizes the way the three are united into one state.

TENNESSEE STATE SEAL

Tennessee's original state seal was designed by a committee of the state legislature in 1801. The seal has gone through some minor changes over the years, but the basic design has stayed the same. At the very top of the seal are the letters XVI, which equals sixteen in **Roman** numerals, signifying that Tennessee was the sixteenth state to join the Union. The seal also highlights the importance of agriculture and commerce to Tennessee's economy.

A common problem in Tennessee is deciding which side of the flag goes up. In 1976 the U.S. Post Office issued a stamp of the flag flying upside down and Tennessee passed a law that explained the proper way to display it.

The current version of the state seal was adopted by the Tennessee General Assembly in 1987.

State Motto: "Agriculture and Commerce"

Tennessee's state motto, "Agriculture and Commerce," is taken from the words that appear on the state seal.

State Nickname: Volunteer State

Tennessee is known as the Volunteer State. It got the nickname because of the thousands of men who **volunteered** to fight for the United States against the British in the **War of 1812.**

State Folk Dance: Square Dance

In 1980 the General Assembly adopted the square dance as Tennessee's state folk dance. In square dancing four couples perform dance moves that are shouted out by a "caller."

"Tennessee Waltz"

I was waltzing with my darlin' to the
   Tennessee Waltz
When an old friend I happened to see
Introduced him to my loved one and while
   they were waltzing
My friend stole my sweetheart from me

I remember the night and the
   Tennessee Waltz
Now I know just how much I have lost
Yes I lost my little darlin' the night they
   were playing
The beautiful Tennessee Waltz.

State Songs

Tennessee has six official state songs, the most of any state. The first one, adopted by the General Assembly in 1925, is "My Homeland, Tennessee." "When It's Iris Time in Tennessee" was added in 1935, followed by "My Tennessee" (the official public school song) twenty years later. Then, in 1965, "Tennessee Waltz" became the fourth state song. "Rocky Top" was adopted in 1982 and "Tennessee" in 1992. Country musicians Pee Wee King and Redd Stewart wrote "Tennessee Waltz." It became a nationwide hit in 1950.

In the spring blooming irises make Tennessee gardens come alive in a blaze of purple.

STATE FLOWERS: PASSION FLOWER AND IRIS

Tennessee has two state flowers. The first is the passion flower, also known as the ocoee. Tennessee schoolchildren chose it as the state flower in 1919. In 1933 the Tennessee General Assembly added a second state flower—the iris. This flower with long petals comes in many different varieties and colors. In 1973 the General Assembly decided that the passion flower would be the state wildflower and the iris the state **cultivated** flower.

STATE TREE: TULIP POPLAR

In 1947 the General Assembly named the tulip poplar Tennessee's state tree. The tulip poplar was chosen because it grows throughout the state and the first settlers used its wood for building. The trees can grow up to 200 feet tall.

The tulip poplar gets its name from its tulip-shaped green and orange flowers.

STATE BIRD: MOCKINGBIRD

In 1933 the people of Tennessee selected the mockingbird as the state bird in a statewide vote. Not only does the mockingbird have its own distinctive song but also it can imitate the songs of other birds.

Some mockingbirds have been heard to bark like a dog.

The Tennessee walking horse is the only horse to be named after a state.

STATE HORSE: TENNESSEE WALKING HORSE

In 2000 the Tennessee General Assembly named the Tennessee walking horse as the official state horse. The horse gets its name from its unusual running walk and because it was first **bred** in Tennessee.

STATE BUTTERFLY: ZEBRA SWALLOWTAIL

The black-and-white-winged zebra swallowtail was named Tennessee's state butterfly in 1995. The zebra swallowtail can be found in the woodlands and fields of Tennessee. It has a wingspan of up to four inches and feeds off **nectar** from blueberry and blackberry flowers.

The zebra swallowtail's caterpillars live and feed on the bottom side of the leaves of the pawpaw tree.

STATE REPTILE: EASTERN BOX TURTLE

In 1995 the General Assembly named the eastern box turtle as the state reptile. With adults measuring about six inches long, these turtles are on the small side. Box turtles live anywhere from 30 to 60 years. Some have even survived to the age of 100.

The eastern box turtle lives in the woods and meadows of Tennessee.

STATE AMPHIBIAN: TENNESSEE CAVE SALAMANDER

In 1995 the General Assembly named the Tennessee cave salamander the official state amphibian. It lives in limestone caves that have streams running through them. These are found mostly in the central and southeastern part of the state.

The Tennessee cave salamander has bright red feathery gills, small eyes, and a large tail fin.

STATE AGRICULTURAL INSECT: HONEYBEE

In 1990 state lawmakers named the honeybee as the official state agricultural insect. Since the honeybee **pollinates** many of Tennessee's crops, including cotton and soybeans, it plays a big role in the state's economy. A beekeeper from Dickson led the campaign to name the honeybee as Tennessee's official agricultural insect.

STATE WILD ANIMAL: RACCOON

The official wild animal of Tennessee is the raccoon, adopted by the General Assembly in 1972. Raccoons make their dens near streams and rivers, where they feed on fish and frogs.

STATE ROCKS: AGATE AND LIMESTONE

In 1969 the General Assembly adopted agate as the state rock. Agate, a type of quartz, is a semiprecious gemstone found mainly in Greene County in the mountains and

Agates are known for their colorful layering and have been used in jewelry for thousands of years.

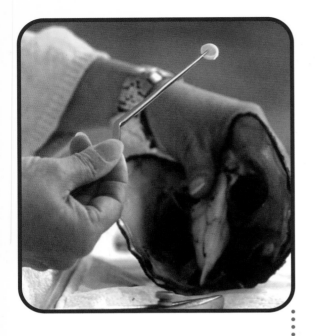

Every year Tennessee exports more than $50 million worth of pearls and mussel shells.

Shelby County near the Mississippi River. In 1979 the General Assembly named a second state rock, limestone. It was chosen because it is commercially valuable and can be found throughout the state.

STATE GEM: FRESHWATER PEARL

The General Assembly adopted the freshwater pearl as the official state gem in 1979. **Mussels** found in Tennessee's rivers sometimes produce pearls. These river pearls do not have the smooth, round look of saltwater pearls. Instead, they come in all sorts of shapes and colors. Today, most pearls in Tennessee come from a pearl farm in Camden, in the western part of the state.

TENNESSEE STATE QUARTER

The 2002 Tennessee quarter commemorates the musical contributions of the Grand Divisions of the state. The guitar honors country music that came out of Nashville, in Middle Tennessee. The trumpet stands for the blues heard in Memphis and West Tennessee. The **fiddle** symbolizes the mountain music of East Tennessee.

The design for Tennessee's state quarter was chosen from more than 1,000 entries in a statewide contest.

Tennessee's History and People

People have lived in Tennessee for thousands of years. Until the 1700s, the residents of the area were all Native American, including the Cherokee, Shawnee, and Creek.

EUROPEAN ARRIVALS

Spanish **conquistadors** such as Hernando de Soto, who passed through in 1541, were the first Europeans to enter what is now Tennessee. It would be more than 100 years before the first European settlers arrived in the area again. In the late 1600s both the British and the French claimed the land and began to build forts there. The region was the site of fighting during the French and Indian War between Britain and France from 1754 to 1763. The British won the war and established their claim to the land that would become Tennessee.

At first, the British tried to keep European settlers from moving into the region. Nevertheless, British colonists from North Carolina and Virginia headed for Tennessee in search of new lands to farm.

Hernando de Soto convinced the king of Spain to allow him to explore and establish colonies in the North American interior.

The first permanent settler was William Bean, who built a farm near the Watauga River in what is now northeastern Tennessee in 1769. Hundreds of other British colonists soon followed. By the early 1770s there were several settlements along the Watauga and other rivers in the east.

At this time, Tennessee was a part of the **colony** of North Carolina. If the colonists needed a judge or any other government official, they had to make a journey of many weeks across the Appalachian Mountains and the lands to the east. To better govern and defend themselves, the settlers formed the Watauga Association in 1772. The Watauga Association was the first example of a **majority-rule government** by European settlers in North America.

By 1779 settlers from the new United States were beginning to move into Middle Tennessee. James Robertson, a **long hunter** familiar with the land, led a group of people to a site on the Cumberland River that would become Nashville. In the first years of the settlement, the settlers came under heavy attack from the Creek and Chickamauga, who saw the newcomers as taking over their land. Many people died on both sides of the conflict.

During the **Revolutionary War** (1775–1783), the Cherokee fought on the side of the

The State of Franklin

In 1784 settlers who were fed up with the North Carolina government's neglect of their region decided to form their own state. They named it Franklin, in honor of Benjamin Franklin. They chose as their governor John Sevier, a **militia** leader in the Watauga Association. Franklin tried to gain admission to the United States but could not get nine of the existing states to approve. In time, the citizens of Franklin argued about the best way to run their state. Because of their lack of unity, North Carolina regained control of the area and established its own government there. By 1788 Franklin had fallen apart.

British. When the British lost, the Cherokee found themselves without powerful friends. Unlike Britain, the United States encouraged its citizens to settle new territories. Many people headed for the sparsely settled and fertile lands of Tennessee.

STATEHOOD

In 1789 North Carolina entered the Union. It had to give up its claim to Tennessee and turn over control of the territory to the U.S. government. By 1795 more than 60,000 people were living in the territory—enough to qualify Tennessee for statehood. On June 1, 1796, Tennessee became the sixteenth state in the Union.

John Sevier was arrested by the state of North Carolina and tried for founding the state of Franklin. He was eventually pardoned by the governor.

Tennessee's population grew to 250,000 people by 1810, and the state became influential in the nation's politics. In 1828 Andrew Jackson became the first Tennessean elected president. During Jackson's presidency, Congress passed the Indian Removal Act of 1830, which stated that the Native American tribes of the Southeast, including the Cherokee of Tennessee, had to leave their lands. In 1838 the U.S. Army forced the Cherokee to walk to their new home in what is now the state of Oklahoma. The hard journey caused the deaths of hundreds of Cherokee. Thousands more died after arriving in their new land. This forced march is now known as the Trail of Tears.

Tennessee also had a problem that would soon divide both the state and the nation. **Slavery** was legal in Tennessee. By 1860 African American slaves made up more than 25 percent of Tennessee's population. Most of these slaves lived in West and Middle Tennessee, where the land was suitable for large-scale farms and **plantations.** East Tennessee, on the other hand, had poorer soil and few slaves.

TENNESSEE IN THE CIVIL WAR

After Abraham Lincoln was elected president of the United States in 1860, slave states including South Carolina, Alabama, and Mississippi began to **secede** from the United States. At first, Tennessee chose to remain in the Union. Most Tennesseans did not think Lincoln's election was worth breaking up the country. But when Lincoln began to organize troops to use against the **Confederacy,** Tennesseans felt that he was going too far. On June 8, 1861, they voted to secede from the Union and join the Confederacy. Tennessee was the eleventh and final state to secede from the Union.

It did not take long for the **Civil War** (1861–1865) to reach Tennessee. In February 1862 Nashville fell to the United States. A few months later, the Union took Memphis.

The Battle of Shiloh was the bloodiest battle of the Civil War. More soldiers died in this one battle than in any other U.S. war combined up to that time.

Tennessee was the site of several major battles during the war. In the Battle of Shiloh in April 1862, the two sides combined suffered a total of 24,000 **casualties.** There was also fierce fighting in the battles of Chickamauga Creek and Chattanooga in late 1863.

After the Civil War Tennessee moved quickly to rejoin the Union. In 1866 the General Assembly approved the Fourteenth Amendment to the U.S. Constitution, which granted **citizenship** to former slaves. Tennessee was the third state to **ratify** it. After ratification, Tennessee was readmitted to the Union.

FAMOUS PEOPLE

Nancy Ward (1738–1824), Cherokee leader. Nan'yehi, Ward's Cherokee name, was born in the Cherokee town of Chota. As a young woman, she earned the title of Ghigau, or "Beloved Woman," because of her bravery in battle. She introduced the Cherokee to European-style weaving and farming. In the early 1800s she tried to stop the Cherokee from selling land to white settlers. She feared that the Cherokee would be forced out of the area. Just a few years after Ward's death, the U.S. Army drove the Cherokee out of their homeland.

Sequoyah's language system had 85 symbols. Each one stood for a different sound in the Cherokee language.

Sequoyah (1776–1843), Cherokee inventor and leader. Sequoyah was born near what is now the town of Vonore. He created a system of writing for the Cherokee. The Cherokee Nation adopted this system in 1821. Because of the respect he gained through his invention, Sequoyah also became one of the tribe's leaders.

Davy Crockett (1786–1836), woodsman and politician. Born in Greene County in eastern Tennessee in 1786, Davy Crockett grew up to be a woodsman, soldier, and politician, serving three terms in the U.S. Congress. One of his best-known sayings was, "Be sure you're right and then go ahead." In 1836 Crockett moved to Texas, where he helped Texans fight for independence from Mexico. He died at the Battle of the Alamo in 1836.

Davy Crockett became famous as a symbol of the toughness and "can-do" spirit that it took to live on the U.S. frontier.

Sam Houston (1793–1863), soldier and politician. Born in Virginia, Houston moved to East Tennessee as a teenager. He served under Andrew Jackson during the War of 1812. After the

war, he served Tennessee as a U.S. congressman from 1823 to 1827 and as governor from 1827 to 1829. When his term ended, Houston moved west. He settled in Texas, where he led the fight for independence from Mexico. Houston served Texas as both governor and senator.

James K. Polk (1795–1849), president. Polk was born in North Carolina but came to Tennessee to follow a career in law and politics. A friend of Andrew Jackson, he served as a U.S. congressman from 1825 to 1839 and as Tennessee's governor from 1839 to 1841. In 1844 he was elected president of the United States.

Andrew Johnson (1808–1875), president. Born to a poor family, Johnson was vice president to Abraham Lincoln in 1864. When Lincoln was assassinated in 1865, Johnson became the seventeenth president of the United States. In 1868 the House of Representatives voted to **impeach** him, mainly because of his sympathetic views toward the South. However, he was able to remain in office by one vote.

Benjamin L. Hooks (1925–), civil rights activist. Born in Memphis, Hooks was a lawyer and an activist in the civil rights movement in Tennessee. In 1965 he became Tennessee's first African American criminal court judge. From 1977 to 1992 he was the executive director of the National Association for the Advancement of Colored People (NAACP), the nation's oldest and largest civil rights organization.

Before entering politics Andrew Johnson owned a tailor shop in Greenville.

Musical Heritage

Music flows through Tennessee. From country music in the mountains, to **gospel** and country in Nashville, to the **blues** and **jazz** in Memphis, Tennessee can offer music to please everyone.

COUNTRY MUSIC

Country music is based on the **folk songs** of the south and the cowboy songs of the west. The name country refers to music's **rural** beginnings. Country music has deep roots in Tennessee. Some people even say that you can find country music's birthplace in Bristol, a city on the Virginia border. In the summer of 1927, Ralph Peer, who worked for a New York City record company, came to Bristol in search of musicians. He set up a recording studio in an old furniture store and waited to see who would come to perform.

The Grand Ole Opry, finished in 1975, can hold up to 4,400 people.

The musicians who came to Peer's studio became some of the first stars of country music. The Carter Family sang, fiddled, and played guitar and the **autoharp.** They later became famous for songs such as "Will the Circle Be Unbroken" and "Wildwood Flower."

In 1925 station WSM in Nashville started broadcasting a live country music show every Saturday

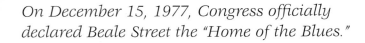

night. One night an announcer introduced the show by telling listeners that they had just finished listening to music taken from "Grand Opera," but they would now listen to the "Grand Ole Opry." The name stuck. Soon other stations began broadcasting the show to homes all across the country. WSM still broadcasts the show today.

THE BLUES

Memphis is home to the blues. The blues was popular in the Mississippi Delta, a region to the south and west of Tennessee. Since Memphis was one of the biggest cities in the area and had a large African American population, Memphis's Beale Street, a major African American business district, became a center for the blues. W.C. Handy, a local musician, made the Memphis blues scene famous in the 1910s with his songs "Memphis Blues" and "Beale Street Blues." Blues clubs lined the street, and people flocked to the area. People still go there to hear the blues today.

The King of Rock and Roll

Elvis Presley made his first records in 1954 at Sun Studios in Memphis. He later became world famous for songs such as "Hound Dog," "Heartbreak Hotel," and "Jailhouse Rock." Presley's **rock and roll** music, which mixed African American rhythm and blues with elements of country music, appealed to a wide audience. His work in creating a whole new musical sound along with his dozens of hit records earned him the nickname "The King of Rock and Roll."

Tennessee's State Government

Like the U.S. government, Tennessee's government is divided into three branches: legislative, executive, and judicial. All three branches of government are centered in Nashville, the state capital.

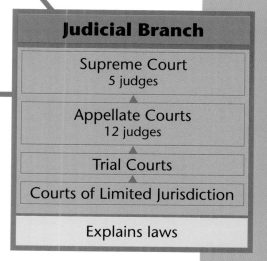

Executive Branch

Governor
(four-year term)

Carries out the laws of the state

Legislative Branch

General Assembly

33 State Senators (four-year term)	99 State Representatives (two-year term)

Makes laws

Judicial Branch

Supreme Court
5 judges

Appellate Courts
12 judges

Trial Courts

Courts of Limited Jurisdiction

Explains laws

LEGISLATIVE BRANCH

The legislative branch is responsible for making laws. Tennessee's legislative branch has a General Assembly made up of elected representatives. Like the U.S. Congress, it is divided into two houses—a house of representatives and a senate.

The house of representatives has 99 members and the senate has 33. The house and the senate each elect a speaker to keep order over legislative sessions. The speaker of the senate also serves as Tennessee's **lieutenant governor.**

Representatives are elected every two years and senators every four years. Their jobs as lawmakers are part-time. The General Assembly meets for 90 days over the course of a 2-year period. For a bill to become law in Tennessee, it has to be passed by a majority in both the house and the senate. If the governor **vetoes** a bill, the General Assembly can override it by another majority.

EXECUTIVE BRANCH

The executive branch enforces the laws. The governor heads the executive branch. The people of Tennessee

Tennessee's capitol building was completed in 1859.

elect a governor every four years. The governor in turn appoints a **cabinet,** which includes the commissioners of 21 state departments. Among them is the Department of Revenue, which is responsible for collecting state taxes. The cabinet also includes the director of the Division of Consumer Affairs. This department works to protect consumers and businesses from unfair business practices.

JUDICIAL BRANCH

The judicial branch interprets and applies the laws of Tennessee. Tennessee's judicial branch has four levels. The lowest level is made up of Courts of Limited **Jurisdiction.** These courts hear cases involving the breaking of city or county laws or **juvenile** cases.

At the next level are the state's four trial courts. Criminal courts deal with cases where the government accuses someone of breaking the law. The Chancery Court handles civil cases, which are brought to court by private citizens instead of by the government. Circuit courts can handle both criminal and civil cases. Also at this level are the probate courts, which handle cases related to wills, instructions that people write telling what to do with their belongings after they die. The third level is the appellate courts, which handle appeals, or requests for new hearings, for both civil and criminal trials.

The Tennessee Supreme Court is the highest court in the state and hears appeals from the lower courts. It also reviews the laws passed by the General Assembly and makes sure that the policies of the executive branch are legal. Supreme Court and appellate court judges are appointed by the governor for an eight-year term. At the end of their term, the people of Tennessee vote on whether to keep them in office. All other judges are chosen through local elections.

Tennessee's Culture

To get a snapshot of Tennessee's culture, you can take a look at some of the many festivals held in the state.

THE NATIONAL STORYTELLING FESTIVAL

More than 30 years ago, a man named Jimmy Neil Smith was listening to the radio when he heard a storyteller spin a tale about going hunting. Smith enjoyed hearing the story, and it gave him an idea—why not start a storytelling festival?

In October 1973 the first National Storytelling Festival was held in Jonesborough, a small mountain town. About 60 people showed up to tell and listen to stories and enjoy the warm fall weather. Over the years crowds grew as more and more people became interested in storytelling. Today, more than 10,000 visitors come to Jonesborough for the festival. The festival organizers set up large tents in the center of the town. People move from tent to tent, listening to whichever storyteller captures their interest.

THE DOGWOOD ARTS FESTIVAL

Knoxville's Dogwood Arts Festival can be traced back to an insult that appeared in a well-known travel

The National Storytelling Festival attracts over 10,000 visitors every autumn to the northeast Tennessee town of Jonesborough.

There are over 60 miles of dogwood trails in Knoxville.

book a long time ago. The author of the book referred to Knoxville as "America's ugliest city." The people of Knoxville were pretty upset, so they decided to prove the author wrong. People in Knoxville had long enjoyed the beauty of the dogwood trees blooming in the spring. They decided to take advantage of this natural beauty and create a set of trails through the parts of the town that had the most dogwoods.

They also created a spring festival to go along with the trails. The Dogwood Arts Festival is held every year in April or May. The Dogwood Arts Festival features traditional arts and crafts. Visitors get a chance to watch baskets being woven and dolls being made from corn **shucks.** Craftspeople such as blacksmiths and quilters also get a chance to display their work.

Elvis Week

One of Tennessee's most unusual cultural events happens every August in Memphis. Elvis fans from around the world stream into Memphis to spend a week celebrating the King of Rock and Roll.

During Elvis Week, fans flock to places that were important to Elvis in his life, such as Sun Studios, where he recorded his first hit records. They enjoy entertainment from Elvis **impersonators** and other musicians. In 2002 there was a big concert that featured people who had played or sung with Elvis when he was alive. Elvis died on August 16, 1977. Every year, during the night of August 16th, fans gather at Graceland, Elvis's mansion and the place he is buried.

29

Tennessee's Food

Tennessee cooking is similar to the cooking found in other southern states. It shows the influence of European and African American culture.

TENNESSEE BREAKFASTS

A traditional Tennessee breakfast always includes biscuits. These light, fluffy, round breads are great for spreading with butter, jam, or honey. Biscuits became popular in the years after the **Civil War** (1861–1865), when inexpensive wheat flour became available for the first time. Some folks put a slice of ham and a ladle-full of red-eye gravy on them. Red-eye gravy comes from the juices of cooked ham boiled with coffee or water. Red-eye gravy gets its name from the red, greasy "eye" that forms on top of the gravy as it cooks.

TENNESSEE SNACKS

One of Tennessee's most famous snacks is the Moon Pie. Originally, the Moon Pie was made from a couple of

Tennessians have been eating Moon Pies for years. They now come in a variety of sizes and flavors.

Ham and Biscuits with Red-Eye Gravy

Always make sure to have an adult work the stove top for you!

Ingredients

1 large center-cut ham slice,
   about ½ inch thick

⅛ teaspoon salt

½ cup water or strong brewed coffee

biscuits, split in half

Directions

Slash fat on edge of ham in several places. Place ham in a hot skillet; brown quickly on each side. Simmer for fifteen minutes or until tender. Remove from pan; keep warm. Sprinkle salt in hot skillet; add coffee or water. Boil for about two minutes. Pour over ham and biscuits.

chocolate-covered graham crackers, with a layer of marshmallow in between. Today, it comes in vanilla and banana flavors, too.

Moon Pies have been made in Chattanooga since 1917. The way the story goes, it was first made as a filling snack that miners could put in their lunch pails. When asked what size snack he wanted, one miner held up his hands around the moon in the sky. Thus, the snack got the name of "Moon Pie."

Tennessee's Folklore and Legends

Legends and folklore are stories that are not totally true but are often based on bits of truth. These stories helped people understand things that could not be easily explained. The earliest known Tennessee folktales come from the Cherokee and other Native Americans who once lived in the area. Later arrivals also had stories to tell. These tales teach the importance of courage, good deeds, and clever thinking in the difficult conditions that the early residents of Tennessee faced.

GRANDMOTHER SPIDER STEALS THE SUN

A long, long time ago, the Cherokee side of the world was completely dark. No one could see a thing, and everyone kept bumping into each other. They needed light, but no one knew how to get it.

Then Fox said that on the other side of the world there were some people who had light. These people were greedy, though, and did not want to share it.

Possum volunteered to steal light from the other side of the world. He said that he could hide it in his bushy tail. So he traveled to the other side of the world and found the sun hanging in a tree. He grabbed a small piece and put it in his tail, but the heat burned all the hair off. When the people on the other side of the world saw what he had done, they took the light back. Possum has had a bald tail ever since.

Finally, Grandmother Spider said she would try. She began by making a thick clay pot. Then she spun a web so long that it reached to the other side of the world. Since Spider was so small, the people on the other side of the world did not notice her. As soon as she arrived, she grabbed the sun, placed it in her clay pot, and hurried home. When she got back with the light, everyone celebrated.

FROZEN DAWN

One winter morning long ago, the weather was so cold that the sunlight froze before it could rise in the sky. When Davy Crockett noticed that morning was slow in coming, he decided to find out what was going on.

Crockett tried to light a fire by striking his fingers together, the way he always did. But the day was so cold, the sparks froze before he could get them to kindle. So he set out without a fire. Crockett walked twenty miles to the top of Daybreak Hill. He discovered that the day was so cold that the earth had actually frozen and could not spin. The sun was stuck between two huge blocks of ice!

Crockett knew that if he did nothing, people all over the world would freeze to death. He pulled a bearskin from his pack and squeezed it until a jet of hot oil squirted out and melted the earth's axis. Then he dumped more oil on the face of the sun to get it unstuck. The earth began turning again, and the sun began to climb into the sky. Crockett picked up his bearskin and walked home, bringing daylight to people with the piece of sunrise he had put in his pocket.

Tennessee's Sports Teams

College sports have been important to people in Tennessee for a long time. Since 1997 major professional teams also have become important to the state. Today, Tennesseeans have plenty of teams to root for.

PROFESSIONAL SPORTS

Major professional sports arrived in Tennessee in 1997, when the Houston Oilers of the National Football League (NFL) moved to the state. The team played in Memphis the first year and then moved to Nashville. Now known as the Tennessee Titans, the team has been one of the best in the NFL over the past few years. In 2000 the Titans played in one of the most exciting Super Bowls ever, losing on the last play of the game.

Nashville also has a National Hockey League (NHL) team. Called the Predators, they took the ice for the first time in the fall of 1998. The Nashville Predators play in the NHL's Southeast Division.

Tennessee's newest professional team is the Memphis Grizzlies of the National Basketball Association (NBA).

Steve McNair, quarterback for the Tennessee Titans, sets up under center against the Houston Texans.

The Vancouver Grizzlies moved to Memphis and began play there in 2002. So for the first time, both Memphis and Nashville have their own major sports teams.

COLLEGE SPORTS

College sports have a long history in Tennessee. The most successful sports teams in the state are at the University of Tennessee, in Knoxville. Its teams, known as the Volunteers, have won many national championships. They have won two national football championships, the most recent occuring in 1998. The school has produced many players for the NFL, including quarterback Peyton Manning. The men's outdoor track and field team has won three national championships, the most recent occurring in 2001.

The Lady Volunteers women's basketball team is a model of excellence. Pat Summitt, the first female coach to win 800 games in the National Collegiate Athletic Association (NCAA), came to Tennessee in 1975. She has coached the Volunteers to six national championships. She also has led the team to ten Southeastern Conference championships and is a member of the National Basketball Hall of Fame.

Tennessee has another team in the Southeastern Conference: the Vanderbilt University Commodores, in Nashville. The third big Tennessee sports school is the University of Memphis, whose teams are known as the Tigers.

Pat Summitt is head coach of the University of Tennessee Lady Volunteers.

Tennessee's Businesses and Products

Since Tennessee's earliest days, many of its residents have farmed or mined for a living. More recently, auto manufacturing and nuclear research facilities have provided jobs to Tennesseans.

MANUFACTURING AND INDUSTRY

Today, industry is important to Tennessee. There have long been large chemical and metal manufacturing businesses in East Tennessee, such as the Eastman chemical plant in Kingsport. More recently, General Motors opened a car manufacturing plant in Spring Hill, and Nissan opened a similar plant in Smyrna.

Tennessee is also home to the Oak Ridge National Laboratory, which is one of the country's most important research centers. Oak Ridge continues to pursue **fusion energy** and other safe and reliable energy resources. The laboratory also includes the National Environmental Research Park, a 35-square-mile area dedicated to finding

Tennessee has become the leading auto manufacturing state in the southeast. Cars from Tennessee's plants are shipped all over the United States.

The TVA's dams have created more than 40 lakes throughout Tennessee.

ways of protecting and managing the environment.

East Tennessee is the most industrialized part of the state thanks to the Tennessee Valley Authority (TVA). President Franklin Roosevelt and the U.S. Congress set up the TVA in the 1930s. The TVA built a series of dams along the Tennessee River to control flooding and produce plenty of **hydroelectric power.** Once the dams were built, they cost relatively little to run and maintain. As a result, the electricity they produced was inexpensive. This made the area a good place to set up factories. It also supplied people living in the area with electricity and jobs.

Today, the TVA is one of the country's largest producers of electricity. It uses 3 nuclear plants, 11 coal plants, 29 dams, and a few other **generators** to provide electricity to more than 8 million people living in and around Tennessee.

FedEx Headquarters in Memphis

Memphis is the world headquarters for the FedEx Corporation. The city was chosen as the headquarters because of its central location in the United States. This package delivery service uses a fleet of more than 600 planes and almost 100,000 trucks and vans to get packages to its customers on time, usually overnight. FedEx started service in 1973 by delivering packages to 25 cities in the United States. Today, it uses more than 200,000 employees to deliver more than 5 million packages a day to more than 200 countries around the world.

The FedEx hub at Memphis keeps packages moving to their destinations 24 hours a day.

Attractions and Landmarks

Tennessee has a great variety of places to visit and things to do. All across the state, there are sites commemorating people and events from throughout the state's history. This chapter highlights the attractions and landmarks in each Grand Division that help make Tennessee unique.

WEST TENNESSEE

On April 4, 1968, **civil rights** leader Martin Luther King Jr. was shot as he stood on the balcony of the Lorraine Motel in Memphis. Today, the hotel is home to the National Civil Rights Museum. The museum tells the story of the civil rights movement through art, multimedia displays, and historical items such as King's speeches.

The National Civil Rights Museum opened in Memphis in 1991.

King's second-floor motel room looks just the way it did on the morning he was shot. Even the cars that King and his companions were using are parked in the lot below. And a new exhibit features the bathroom across the street from which the assassin shot King as he stood on the motel balcony.

One of the most famous attractions in Memphis is Graceland, Elvis Presley's former home. Presley lived here from 1957 until his death twenty years later. Today, it is a shrine for Elvis fans. Visitors to Graceland can see not only Elvis's home but also his car collection, including a Ferrari and a pink Cadillac.

Graceland was named after the previous owner's aunt, a woman named Grace Toof.

Places to See in Tennessee

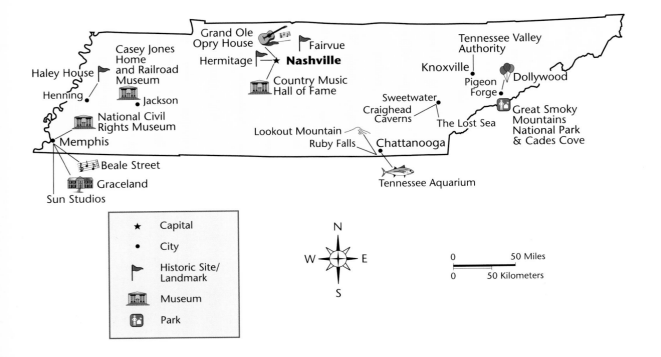

In a house in Henning, a small town outside of Memphis, Alex Haley first heard the stories that inspired him to search for his roots in Africa. The house was owned by his mother's parents, and Haley used to spend his summers visiting them. His grandmother would tell him stories about his **ancestors,** including the story of Kunta Kinte, a young man who was brought over from Africa as a slave in 1767. When he grew up, Haley became a writer and wrote a book about his family's heritage. The book *Roots* won the **Pulitzer Prize** in 1977. Today, the house is open as a museum, furnished to look the way it did when Haley was born. The museum also includes information about the people on whom Haley based his characters in *Roots*.

The Casey Jones Home and Railroad Museum in Jackson is a shrine to a U.S. folk hero. Casey Jones was a train engineer who died in a major train wreck in Mississippi in 1900 while trying to save the lives of his passengers. Wallace Saunders, an African American who worked as an engine wiper for the railroad, wrote a song about the crash, and Casey became famous. The museum includes Casey's home and a model of the site of the fatal accident. Also at the museum is an old steam engine much like the one Casey was driving when he crashed.

MIDDLE TENNESSEE

The Hermitage, located outside of Nashville, was the home of Andrew Jackson, the first Tennessean to be elected president of the United States. Jackson built the mansion in 1819 and rebuilt it after a fire that happened while he was president. Today, the mansion is a museum and is furnished the same way it was when Jackson was alive, including a leather chair once owned by George Washington. Also at the site are slave quarters, formal gardens, and the original log cabins that Jackson lived in before the mansion was built. Jackson and his wife Rachel are buried in a cemetery there.

Isaac Franklin made a fortune buying and selling other human beings. Franklin was an owner of the largest slave-trading company in the United States in the early 1800s. With

The Hermitage displays many of Jackson's personal belongings, including his sword and his Bible.

the money he made from his business, he built a mansion outside of Nashville in 1832. He called his new home Fairvue. The 11,000-square-foot mansion is recognized as a National Historic Landmark because it is a good example of an antebellum, or pre–**Civil War,** plantation.

EAST TENNESSEE

The most visited national park in the country sits on the border of Tennessee and North Carolina. Great Smoky Mountains National Park attracts nearly ten million visitors a year. The mountains get their name from the blue-gray mist that often covers

The Cherokee tribe called eastern Tennessee "The Land of a Thousand Smokes" because of the smoky haze that hovers over the mountains.

them. The park is 800 square miles in size, and forest covers about 95 percent of the land. Clingman's Dome, which at 6,643 feet is the highest peak in Tennessee, can be found in the park. On a clear day, visitors can see more than 100 miles from the observation tower at the top of the mountain. The park even has a **ghost town.** When the park was established, the residents of Cades Cove had to pack up and leave. Today, the buildings remain as an open-air museum of mountain life in the 1800s.

In 1986 country singer Dolly Parton bought a small amusement park in Pigeon Forge, near her hometown. She renamed the park Dollywood, and Pigeon Forge has not been the same since. Dollywood combines rides, examples of old-time mountain living such as a one-room schoolhouse, and scenes from Parton's life such as a rebuilt version of her childhood home. Its location near the Great Smoky Mountains National Park helps draw visitors. More than two million people a year come to enjoy the amusement park and enjoy the mountain scenery that surrounds it.

One of the state's newest attractions is the Tennessee Aquarium. It opened in 1992 in a modern building in downtown Chattanooga. The

The roller coaster at Dollywood, called the Tennessee Tornado, drops 128 feet while going 70 miles per hour.

Catfish live near the bottom of many of Tennessee's rivers. The blue catfish, shown here, can grow to as much as 150 pounds.

aquarium has the largest collection of freshwater aquatic life in the country, with more than 9,000 animals in all. When visitors arrive at the aquarium, they take an elevator ride to the top. From there, they can take their time exploring the twelve stories of exhibits and indoor habitats, such as a 60-foot deep canyon and two indoor forests. It takes a lot of water to give all those animals room to swim—about 400,000 gallons worth!

Map of Tennessee

Reelfoot Lake

Mississippi River

West Tennessee

Kentucky Lake

Oak Ridge

Camden

Dickson

Tennessee River

Bakerville

Middle Tennessee

Cumberland River

★ Nashville

Smyrna

Spring Hill

Cumberland Plateau

Knoxville

Sweetwater

Chota

Vonore

Eastern Tennessee

Johnson City

Appalachian Mountains

GREENE COUNTY

Watauga River

Bristol

Clingmans Dome 6,643 ft

Great Smoky Mountains

SHELBY COUNTY

Memphis

Shiloh

Chattanooga

Tennessee River

Chickamauga Creek

ILLINOIS
IND.
OHIO
W. VA.
MISSOURI
KENTUCKY
VA.
Nashville
★
TENNESSEE
N.C.
ARK.
S.C.
MISS.
ALABAMA
GEORGIA

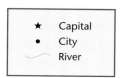

★ Capital
• City
〰 River

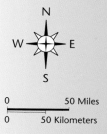

N
W — E
S

0   50 Miles
0   50 Kilometers

Glossary

ancestors direct relatives who lived long ago

atom bomb a bomb that creates an explosion by splitting atoms to release energy

autoharp a stringed musical instrument that you play by strumming

blues a style of music developed from African American folk songs

bluffs low cliffs

bred raised animals under conditions that allowed people control of the traits the animals inherited

cabinet a group of elected or appointed officials that advise a governor or other executive

casualties someone who is seriously injured or killed in an accident

citizenship full membership in a city, state, or country

civil rights relating to court action between individuals having to do with private rights rather than criminal action

Civil War (1861–1865) the American war between the Northern states and the Southern states

colony a group of people who settle in a distant land but remain under the authority of their homeland's government

Confederacy the eleven slave-holding states that left the United States in 1860 and 1861

conquistadors Spanish soldiers who explored and conquered parts of the Americas

cultivated grown through the efforts of gardeners and farmers

fiddle a violin

folk songs songs traditionally sung by the people who live in a country or region

fusion energy energy created by combining two atoms into one

generators machines that create electricity

ghost town a town that has been left by all its residents

gospel a style of American religious music, originally based on folk songs

hydroelectric power electricity generated by the flow of water

impersonator a person who takes on the appearance or character of someone else

impeach to charge a public official with misconduct in office

jazz an American musical style in which musicians make up melodies that are variations of the main melody

jurisdiction the power to apply the law

juvenile not yet an adult

lieutenant governor the second highest official in the executive branch, who takes over for the governor if necessary

long hunter on the frontier, a hunter who went off for extended trips, sometimes lasting over a year

majority-rule government a system where the decision made by more than half of a group of voters applies to the entire group

militia an army of ordinary people, not professional soldiers

mussels a type of shellfish with dark blue shells

nectar a sweet liquid in some flowers

nuclear energy energy that comes from splitting or joining atoms

nuclear reactor a device that splits atoms to generate power

plantations large farms worked by slaves

plutonium a powerful, dangerous metal that is generated by some nuclear reactors

pollinates uses pollen to fertilize a flower

precipitation water that falls from the sky

Pulitzer Prize annual award given to people who excel in journalism, literature, music, and the arts

ratify to approve something

Revolutionary War war that the Thirteen Colonies fought from 1775 to 1783 for independence from Great Britain

rock and roll a form of popular music with a strong beat and electrified instruments

Roman member of the ancient Roman Empire

rural relating to the country

secede to declare that you are no longer part of a country or organization

shucks the outer covering

slavery the practice of one human being being owned by another

temperate having temperatures and weather that are neither very hot nor very cold

uranium a silvery metal that is used in nuclear reactors

vetoes overrules a law passed by the legislative branch

volunteered offered to join the military

War of 1812 a war between Great Britain and the United States fought from 1812 to 1815

World War II a war fought from 1939 to 1945 in which Great Britain, France, the Soviet Union, the United States, and their allies defeated Germany, Italy, and Japan

More Books to Read

Alphin, Elaine Marie. *Davy Crockett.* Minneapolis, Minn.: Lerner Publications Co., 2003.

Burke, Rick. *Andrew Jackson (American Lives: Presidents).* Chicago: Heinemann, 2002.

Kent, Deborah. *Tennessee (America the Beautiful, Second Series).* Chicago: Children's Press, 2001.

Weatherly, Myra S. *Tennessee.* New York: Children's Press, 2001.

Wilcox, Charlotte. *The Tennessee Walking Horse (Learning about Horses).* Mankato, Minn.: Capstone Press, 1996.

Index

About the Author

Adam McClellan grew up spending his summers in the Blue Ridge Mountains on Tennessee's border with North Carolina. He will be forever grateful to Tennessee for giving the world both country music and Memphis blues. Adam lives in Chapel Hill with his wife and daughter.